40 DAYS

TRANSFORMED BY THE TRUTH

Tabitha Thomas

"You shall know the truth and the truth shall set you free."
John 8:32

Published by
Yellow Dog Publishing

All rights reserved.
No part of this book may be reproduced in any form, by photocopying or any electronic or mechanical means, including information storage or retrieval systems, without permission in writing from the copyright owner and the book's publisher.

First published August 2024
Copyright © Tabitha Thomas 2024

Cover design – Brendan Conboy
Illustrations – Brendan Conboy

Printed in Great Britain

*40 Days journey
of transformation and
drawing near to God*

Dedication

Transformed by the Truth is a devotional book dedicated to all women. It teaches how to seek the heart of the Father by dwelling in his presence and to live by faith, not by sight; by allowing the truth of the word to transform the mind, soul and heart and find intimacy with the Father.

About the Author

Tabitha Thomas is a dedicated missionary and social responsibility coordinator known for her unwavering faith and commitment to reaching out to communities and inspiring the next generation. Her journey reflects a deep reliance on God and a passion for making a positive impact globally.

Early Career and Call to Missionary Work

For five years, Tabitha worked as a pharmacist in Tanzania. However, feeling a divine call to serve more communities, she resigned from her position and moved to South Africa in 2017. There, she pursued further studies in social sciences and counselling. Her initial intention was to enhance her skills, but God had a greater plan. Tabitha ended up working full-time in ministry and furthered her studies in ministry as well, dedicating seven years to community outreach and social responsibility projects.

Inspiring Women and Building Movements

Throughout her life, Tabitha has been passionate about inspiring women to develop intimate relationships with God. She organised various retreats and prayer sessions, including mountain prayers and online gatherings, to support women growing in their faith and purpose.

In her twenties, Tabitha started a movement in Tanzania called 'Ladies of Faith and Ladies of Destiny.' This initiative gathered women to pray for their families and futures. When she moved to South Africa, she founded another movement called 'Ladies Retreat,' which brought women together to seek God's heart and grow in love and support for one another.

Ministry and Community Work

Tabitha's ministry work in South Africa involved extensive community outreach, focusing on social responsibility projects. She aimed to inspire both young and old women to live lives of purpose and faith, supporting them in their spiritual growth and helping them step out in faith even in challenging situations.

Current Mission in the United Kingdom

In 2023, Tabitha felt called to the United Kingdom as her next mission field. She is now pursuing her calling as a missionary, productive life coach, and social responsibility coordinator. Partnering with charities, she works to bring hope and God's love to communities in need.

Tabitha's journey continues to be driven by her joy in seeing women walk in freedom, embrace their God-given identities, and support one another in love and faith. Her story is a testament to living a life of purpose and faith, dedicated to serving others and fulfilling God's calling.

Table of content

1. Be still in Me
2. Trust Me, I will help you
3. Do not allow your heart to be troubled
4. He is faithful to calm your storm
5. Dwell in Me
6. Keep waiting on Me
7. Rise up and take courage
8. The truth shall set you free
9. I am watching over you
10. I will be with you
11. Live life worthy of My call
12. Do not be afraid
13. My time is coming
14. I got your back
15. Surrender to Me
16. Grateful heart
17. Teach me Your ways
18. I will fight for you
19. My grace is sufficient for you
20. Rest in Me
21. Transformed by the truth

22 Take a step of faith
23 Learn to let go and let God in
24 Believe in Me
25 Do not give up
26 I will level the mountains
27 Be the light
28 The Lord Is my Rock & and my Fortress
29 Nothing is impossible
30 Learn from Me
31 Rejoice in Me
32 Trust My ways, not yours
33 Don't forget who you are
34 The best Is yet to come
35 Seek to know Me
36 Give Me your burden
37 Draw near to Me
38 I love you with unending love
39 Hear My voice
40 You are free indeed

Day 1
Be still in me

Psalm 46:10
Be still and know I am God.

Often, we find ourselves overwhelmed in life and struggle with the many battles we face. Our hearts feel troubled and disconnected from our loving relationship with the Father. But today, God is sending an invitation to you, to choose to be still in Him; regardless of the circumstances and what you're going through. He wants you to rest in Him. Let go of your pain, your disappointment, and all the overwhelming things.

Just because you feel things are difficult. does not mean God does not see you. He sees you and He

wants you to choose to rest in Him "
I hear Jesus say, "Give to Me, I can handle it, don't carry it alone."

APPLICATION
Take a few minutes, breathe in and out and rest in His presence. During your quiet time, listen for God's voice and write down what you hear from Him.

DECLARATION
Lord, thank You for allowing me to rest in You and hear Your voice today. I choose to rest in You and give You all the things that overwhelm me. I give You all my pain, all my burdens, all my hurt with my praise for You. I declare from today I will rest in Your love and choose to be still in You.

In Jesus' name, I pray, amen.

Further scriptures:
Matthew 11:28-29
1 Peter 5:6-7

Use this space to journal your thoughts.

Day 2
Trust me, I will help you

Isaiah 41:13
For I am the Lord your God who takes hold of your right hand and says to you, "Do not fear I will help you."

There are many things in life to celebrate and rejoice in. When times are difficult with no breakthrough in sight, people tend to give up hope and stop pursuing what they've trusted. It can feel like walking alone in the desert.

Today, I want you to open your ears and listen to God's voice. Is He encouraging you to take another step of faith and trust Him? Is He reaching out His hand to pull you up?

I hear God say, "Trust Me, I will help you, hold My hand tight and walk with Me, I will teach you. I will lead you on the path you should go."

APPLICATION
Take a moment in a quiet time and write down the things you feel are hard. Write down how you feel. If you're scared to continue, ask God to give you a brave heart and trust Him again.

DECLARATION
Lord, thank You for always being with me, and helping me to take steps of faith, even when I feel scared. Today I choose to trust You and fully depend on You. I declare Your peace and trust You'll lead me in all I do. I'll follow Your steps, not my plan.

In Jesus' name, amen.

Further scriptures
Proverb 3:5
Psalm 32:8

Use this space to journal your thoughts.

Day 3
Do not allow your heart to be troubled

John 14:27
"Peace I leave with you, My peace I give to you, let not your heart be troubled, neither let them be afraid."

Peace is something we can take for granted. Often the world brings things into our lives which can trouble our peace. We can forget to pray because our hearts are troubled.

If we allow our hearts to be troubled, we open doors for the enemy to steal our joy and peace.

Today, Jesus wants you to remember the moment

you allowed your heart to be troubled and made a wrong decision. Ask Him to fill you with an abundance of peace and take everything that troubles your heart. Whether it be friendship, marriage, work, family or anything else, Jesus wants you to bring it to His feet.

I hear God say, "Give to Me all things that are troubling you, I will give you rest and an abundance of peace, let go of your pain and take My peace."

APPLICATION
As you take a moment to reflect on the things that troubled you today, write down everything you want to give to Jesus and think of every person who you need to forgive, then allow your heart to be free so that you can receive God's peace.

DECLARATION
Dear Lord, thank You for the divine peace that You pour out to me, helping me to access Your presence. I declare peace abundantly over my life, my relationships, my family, my workplace, and all areas of my life.

In Jesus' name, amen.

Further scriptures
Psalm 29:1 1
Isaiah 26:3

Use this space to journal your thoughts.

Day 4
He is faithful to calm your storm

Matthew 8:26
Then He got up and rebuked the winds and the waves and it was completely calm.

Jesus can calm the storms of life. If we invite Him to be with us in all seasons, He can calm the storm that you're facing right now.

When we're surrounded by challenges that feel like storms, we can feel lonely, like we need to fight the battle alone similar to how the disciples felt in the boat when they forgot Jesus was with them.

Today, Jesus invites you to wake up and face the storm with Him. He is there to help you and will calm your storm. He wants you to feel His love and his presence.

Just because you feel your life is facing the storms, doesn't mean that Jesus is not with you. Take courage and invite Jesus to help you to calm your storm.

I hear God saying, "I am greater than any storm you are facing right now, I am who I am. I am with you to help you to calm the storm. Invite me into your storm and I will give you peace that surpasses all your understanding."

APPLICATION
Spend a few moments in God's presence and think of the storms you face in this season. Speak peace and healing into that area, allow God's peace to fill you and ask for his peace to calm the storm you're facing.

DECLARATION
Dear, precious Daddy, help me to invite You to calm my storm, to take over and give me peace. I want to feel Your presence and Your love in this

season and believe You are bigger than the storm I'm facing.

In Jesus' name, amen

Further scriptures:
Matthew 11:28-29,
Isaiah 43:18-19

Use this space to journal your thoughts.

Day 5
Dwell in Me

Psalm 27:4
One thing I ask from the Lord, this only I ask, that I may dwell in the house of the Lord all the days of my life.

Our lives are surrounded by busy schedules that place obstacles in front of our time with God. This can lead us to feel spiritually dry and outside of God's presence.

Today's devotion is a call to remind you, that God's presence is available for you to access. Jesus invites us to dwell in His presence and feel His love, peace, and joy.

If we do not invite Him as we start our day, we might feel He is far from us throughout the day. He is always available and ready to give us His love and peace.

I hear God say, "Invite Me in and walk with Me, all the time and you will feel My presence, I'm always with you to comfort you and teach you the way you should go."

APPLICATION
Today I want you to write your plans with Jesus and invite His presence to walk with you. In your quiet time, spend a few minutes to feel His love and presence over your life.

DECLARATION
Dear, my precious Daddy, I invite Your presence into my life today. I repent for the time I walk alone without inviting Your presence. Today, I declare Your presence to follow me in my workplace, my family, and all I do.

In Jesus name, amen

Further scriptures:
Exodus 33:14
Jeremiah 29:12-13

Use this space to journal your thoughts.

Day 6
Keep waiting on Me

Isaiah 40:31
But those who hope in the Lord will renew their strength. They will soar on wings like eagles, they will run and not grow weary, they will walk and not faint.

Waiting is not an easy task. We often become tired when waiting. Many of us will grow weary and faint when waiting.

As you meditate on today's devotion, I want you to pray for God to give you renewed strength, especially if you feel you have been waiting long.

Today I have questions I want you to think about.

How are you waiting?
Are you waiting in hope?
Does your waiting season still glorify God?

If you can answer these questions and be honest before the Father, you will experience the freedom not to give up on your waiting.

I sense that God wants to restore hope as you wait on things which you have felt you want to give up on.

I hear God say, "My promise still stands; I will do what I promised. I will do it. Just continue waiting on Me patiently and believe I will come for you."

APPLICATION
In reflection on today's word, I want to think of the things you have been waiting for. If it seems overwhelming or you want to give up, I want you to write down those things in your diary. Ask God to give you fresh hope and new strength as you wait on Him whose promises are faithful.

DECLARATION

Dear, my precious Father, help me to trust Your promises even if the environment doesn't make sense. I pray for a new strength today as I wait for You. Refresh my hopes and my dreams. I trust You, Lord, that You will finish what You started on me.

In Jesus' name, amen.

Further scriptures:
Lamentations 3:25
Habakkuk 2:3

Use this space to journal your thoughts

Day 7
Rise up and take courage

Hebrews 13:6
The Lord is my helper; I will not be afraid.

We're surrounded by many challenges and difficulties in our lives. Sometimes you may feel lonely in the situation you're facing. Even the disciples forgot that Jesus was there when He was with them in person. Do you feel lonely with a troubled heart or feel overwhelmed with what is going on?

I hear God saying to you today, "I am here with you, you are not alone in what you're going through. Be still in Me and trust the process I am taking you through, it's all for your good. Rise up and take courage, I will help you and hold you with MKy right hand."

APPLICATION
Think of times your heart was troubled and did not feel peace. Take a minute and think of the current situation you're facing. I want you to imagine being in a boat with Jesus like the disciples were. I want you to invite Jesus to calm your storm and give you the courage to continue. Rest in quiet time, breathe in and out, and allow God's peace and calm Spirit to cover you. Allow yourself to be still in His presence and ask Him to give you new strength.

DECLARATION
Dear, precious Father, thanks for calming my situation and giving me courage. Help me to choose to be still in You no matter what I'm facing. I declare abundant peace over my soul and believe You will fight for me, and I will be still. Restore my hope and give me the courage to continue looking to You and not give up.

In Jesus name, amen.

Further scriptures
Exodus 14:14
Luke 8:22-25

Use this space to journal your thoughts

Day 8
The truth shall set you free

John 8:32
"Then you will know the truth and the truth will set you free."

God's word is the truth that the Bible wants us to dwell in, knowing the perfect will of the Father's heart for us allows us to live a life of freedom. I sense God's love inviting you to His presence and knowing His word is truth, will set you free from all addiction, sickness, or anything that draws you back. Trust and give thanks for your complete healing and restoration.

God's arms are always open wide to receive us and embrace us to live a life of freedom, even in our mess, His love is persistent and pursues us.

APPLICATION
Today's devotion is challenging you to let go of your struggles and give to Jesus to set you free. Think of something you have been struggling with over the years in which you want to receive freedom. Speak of that struggle to Jesus and ask for forgiveness for dwelling on your own strength to overcome and thank Him for releasing you of your burdens.

DECLARATION
Lord Jesus, I declare today I am free and renounce the enemy. I am free indeed because Jesus paid all the price for my freedom. I will continue to love, serve and remain in the world in freedom.

In Jesus' name, amen.

Further scriptures
Romans 6:22
James 4:7-8

Use this space to journal your thoughts

Day 9
I am watching over you

Psalm 91:14
"Because he loves me," says the Lord, "I will rescue him, I will protect him, I will be with him in trouble, I will deliver him and honour him."

God's love for us is beyond what we feel or see with our eyes. His protection over our lives is more than we see in this limited physical realm. His promise for our lives is 'Yes and Amen.'

I sense God speaking to your heart right now. Spirit of fear and attacks from the enemy over your life will cease. You're free because Christ set you free.

God's eyes are watching over us.

APPLICATION
Pray for God's protection over your life, future, and anything that brings fear. If you feel attacks from the enemy, call upon the blood of Jesus and give thanks for your freedom and deliverance.

DECLARATION
Dear, my precious Father, I declare protection over my life. I pray for my family, and my future and declare restoration of every place in my life. I stop the attacks from the enemy, he has no access to me in any way. My present and my future are protected by the blood of Jesus. The blood of the Lamb covers my family and household. I'm victorious and more than a conqueror.

In Jesus name, amen.

Further scriptures
1 Corinthians 10:13
2 Thessalonians 3:3

Use this space to journal your thoughts

Day 10
I will be with you always

Hebrews 13:5
"Never will I leave you, nor will I forsake you."

God promises to remain with us in every season. Often, we feel lonely or feel we're walking alone through difficult times. We tend to forget the promise that God has given – that he will never leave us.

In our fleshly body, we're prone to feeling lonely. This is an opportunity to invite Jesus to reign over your feelings and emotions for you to feel the love of the Father amid the challenges you are facing.

I hear God say, "I will be with you always to help

you and hold your hand tight. Trust My will not yours. I will never leave you, not forsake you. Hear My voice and walk in the direction I will show you. My eyes will guide you in each step."

APPLICATION
Take a moment to think of when you felt alone and overwhelmed. Allow Jesus to come and reign over your situation. The same as the woman with the issue of blood who touched the garment of Jesus, to feel His presence and received healing in her soul.

DECLARATION
Lord Jesus, thanks for always being with me, I declare: May your Holy Spirit cover me and always fill me with Your power so that I feel Your love and presence all the days of my life.

In Jesus name, amen.

Further scripture
Isaiah 41:10
Matthew 28:20

Use this space to journal your thoughts

Day 11
Live life worthy of my calling

Philippians 1:21
For me to live is Christ and to die is gain.

Paul encourages us in his letter to live a life worthy of our calling and see how we touch the lives of people in the season God entrusted you here on Earth.

Often, we get frustrated when we do not live a life of purpose. We might keep changing jobs, lifestyles or friendship groups when attempting to fill the void of not knowing or walking out the unique purpose God assigned to us. Remember, you are who God says you are. Nothing in this world will give you true identity or purpose. You are unique, fearless and the loving creation of God Almighty.

I hear God say, "I love you just as you are, don't allow the enemy to speak otherwise. You are wonderful and fearfully made. I created you and want to use you for My purpose. Rise and take courage to be who I called you to be."

APPLICATION

Write down your gifts/talents. Ask the Holy Spirit to show you where you have been using your gifts and talents, and then thank God for using you to touch lives. Evaluate how you improve and live a life worthy of your calling in an area you are fearful to walk. Ask God to make you who He called you to be.

PRAYER

Dear, precious Father, help me embrace life and live worthy of my calling. I pray I will live to the full capacity of who You called me to be. The Holy Spirit gives me a spirit of boldness to allow You to use my gifts and talents and advance Your kingdom.

In Jesus' name, amen.

Further scriptures
Galatians 2:20
Philippians 1:20

Use this space to journal your thoughts

Day 12
Do not be afraid

Isaiah 41:10
"Do not fear, for I am with you do not be dismayed for I am your God, I will strengthen you and help you, I will help you."

Many battles we face are a plan of the enemy to bring fear and worry and take our focus off God. As women, God blessed us with a gift of courage and today, Jesus invites you to change your worry into worship and your pain into praise. Just as an aeroplane takes to the sky, it goes against the wind. God wants us to raise our voice of praise and go against our fear and our worry. That is how we conquer the enemy. We're not alone when we feel fear. Remember that Jesus is with you when you fight your battles.

I hear God saying, "Give to Me all things that make you feel overwhelmed and give Me all your fear and worry. Rest in Me and you will find peace in Me."

APPLICATION
Today's application needs you to think about the things you fear. Mention everything that brings worry into your heart and spend quiet time asking God to fill you with new power and a spirit of faith. Ask God to exchange your strength with His.

PRAYER
Thank You, Lord, for the spirit of faith and sound mind. I pray today for any spirit of fear or worry to not control my life. I invite You, Jesus, to give me the boldness to do all things through You, Christ who strengthens me.

In Jesus name, amen.

Further scriptures
Philippians 4:13
2 Timothy 1:7

Use this space to journal your thoughts

Day 13
My time is coming

John 2:4
Jesus said unto her, "Woman, what have I to do with you? Mine hour has not yet come."

As women, we tend to rush and want everything in place as soon we see a need. As with Jesus' mother, she wished Jesus to perform miracles before His appointed time. I know there are many things you might trust God to do in your life and sometimes you pray for God to intervene, even if the time is not right.

Today's devotion reminds us that God's time is the best and perfect time and when the time is right God will do what He promised.

I hear God saying, "My time is perfect and I always give good gifts to those I love, wait on Me patiently and learn to wait on My time.

APPLICATION
Think about something you've been wanting for Jesus to do for you, that you feel He is delaying to come through for you. Write down in your journal and ask Jesus to give you the grace to wait on His time.

PRAYER
Dear, my precious Father, help me to wait on You, teach me to wait on Your time even when I want things to happen in my way. I surrender all my needs and my desires to you.

In Jesus name, I pray, amen.

Further scriptures
Ecclesiastes 3:11
Jeremiah 29:11

Use this space to journal your thoughts

Day 14
I got your back

Isaiah 43:19
"Behold, I will do a new thing; now it shall spring forth; shall ye not know it? I will even make a way in the wilderness, and rivers in the desert."

Sometimes life brings us to places where we feel overwhelmed; as if we're walking in the wilderness. Perhaps, the situation you're facing can be likened to walking in the desert. As women, we tend to cry in times of frustration, anxiety and pain. Especially, if we lack certainty about our future, sometimes we feel like giving up. Today in this devotion God promises to be with you when you walk in the wilderness. You don't need to feel alone or give up on your dreams.

I hear God saying, "Trust Me in this season. It looks like everything is not going to plan but I want you to trust My plans, not yours, My will not yours."

APPLICATION
Find a quiet place. Breathe in and out and allow the Holy Spirit to breathe new hope into you. Invite Jesus to walk with you in the desert because you don't want to walk alone.

PRAYER
Dear, my precious Father, help me to surrender all my plans. Allow me to walk with You, even though I don't see a way, I will trust You to make a way in the wilderness just as You promised.

In Jesus name, I pray, amen.

Further scriptures
Psalm 23:1-6
Psalm 138:4

Use this space to journal your thoughts

Day 15
Surrender to Me

Matthew 11:28
"Come unto Me, all ye that labour and are heavily laden, and I will give you rest."

Jesus is inviting you to be in a place of rest and enjoy your loving relationship with Him. As women, we can carry many things and work on several projects simultaneously, but do we forget to rest in God? Our love for Jesus leads to obedience and surrender, enabling us to live under His Lordship. Even though life brings overwhelming challenges, Jesus calls us to lay everything at His feet and to rest in Him. We get overwhelmed with things in this world, as we try to carry everything that Jesus called us to surrender to Him.

APPLICATION
Today's word encourages you to rest in God and learn to give to Jesus all things that overwhelm you. As you journal today, mention everything you need to submit and surrender to Jesus. Ask Him to give you rest.

PRAYER
Dear, my precious Father, today I surrender everything that I can't handle. I choose to surrender everything that is overwhelming me. Give me rest and peace.

In Jesus name, I pray, amen.

Further scriptures
1 Peter 5: 7
Psalm 34:18

Use this space to journal your thoughts

Day 16
Grateful heart

Psalm 150
Praise God in His sanctuary, praise Him in His mighty heavens. Praise Him for his acts of power, praise Him for His surpassing greatness.

When life brings challenges or trouble, we tend to focus on the negative and forget the great things God enabled us to overcome. Today's meditation invites us into a place of gratitude, like David, who always knew of the goodness of God and wrote the psalm of praise. If you're going through difficulties, don't stop praising God for what He has done and is going to do in your life. I sense the Holy Spirit reminding you today of what He already overcame with you. You have the assurance, that He will do it again, as you raise your head to praise Him and continue to have a heart of gratitude.

The heart of gratitude opens doors for God to do more than you ask for.

APPLICATION
As you apply the heart of gratitude today, I want you to write all the mountains that God helped you to move or overcome. I want you, to mention the mountains you face in this season. Spend time in prayer with thanksgiving, trust God will do it again.

PRAYER
Dear, Heavenly Father, thanks for Your love, mercy, and all You have done in my life. Thanks for the gift of life and all the answered prayers. Today, I raise my voice of praise, I thank You for what You have done and what You are going to do.

In Jesus name, I pray, amen.

Further scriptures
Psalm 136
Psalm 138

Use this space to journal your thoughts

Day 17
Teach me Your way

Psalm 32:8
"I will instruct and teach you in the way you should go. My eyes will guide you."

Of all life's decisions, sometimes we make good choices and sometimes bad choices. In today's word, God, the Father invites us to rely on His way, His direction. He promises to direct us and His eyes will guide us. Women were created differently from men and have different roles. When we carry many things, we tend to rely on our own strength, which usually leads to feeling overwhelmed, especially if it doesn't go according to plan.

Mistakes are the lessons for a person who will grow. They enable us to become wiser and more prudent, to avoid making those same mistakes. I hear God saying, "You tried many times and did not get the results you always wanted. I invite you to hold My hand and this time choose to walk with Me and don't walk alone. Hear My voice and follow My steps."

APPLICATION
Journal things you've attempted but didn't get the results you hoped or expected. Spend a quiet time and hear God's direction for all you're trusting from Him.

PRAYER
Dear, my precious Father, today I surrender all my plans, my dreams and all of my ways to You. Teach me Your way and lead me to the path You want me to take. I repent for all the time I used my own thoughts and my own ways to do things. I invite You to lead in the way I should go. Please, guide me with Your eyes.

In Jesus name, amen.

Further scriptures
Proverb 3:5
Psalm 23:4

Use this space to journal your thoughts

In Jesus name, I pray, amen.

Further scriptures
1 Corinthians 16:13-14
Psalm 59:16

Use this space to journal your thoughts

Day 20
Rest in Me

Matthew 11:28
"Come unto me, all ye that labour and are heavy laden, and I will give you rest."

Rest is vital for a spirit. To be in a calm space that will help your mental well-being. Even though life gives us fatigue and causes us to feel overwhelmed, Jesus invites us to be in a place of rest. Rest in Him with the assurance He has you covered, and cast away the stress of your debts and everything you have not yet accomplished.

I hear God saying today, "Come just as you are, I will give you peace, and even in your overwhelming schedules, I will teach you to work from a place of rest. Everything that overwhelms you, give it to Me. I can handle it, don't try to fix it in your own strength, I will help you. Just trust Me to walk with you."

APPLICATION

In your quiet time today, I want you to practice breathing in and out seven times and imagine the walls of Jericho falling. Anything that is currently overwhelming you or pressing on your heart, give it to Jesus. He'll take the weight off your shoulders and give you peace, His calming spirit will enable you to rest in Him.

PRAYER

Dear, precious Father, today I choose to give You everything that is pressing on me, I receive Your peace and calm spirit. Even in my battles and challenges, I choose to remain calm with the assurance that You're with me and will give me rest in the middle of any situation I'm facing. Breathe Your calm spirit into me and give me rest.

In Jesus name, amen.

Further scriptures
Psalm 29:11
2 Thessalonians 3:3

Use this space to journal your thoughts

Day 21
Transformed by the truth

John 8:32
"And ye shall know the truth, and the truth shall make you free."

As you finish week three with God, remember your true identity and who He called you to be as a woman of character, ready to transform the lives of those around you.

Today's devotion reminds you to continue dwelling in God's word, for your mind and spirit to be transformed. If anything, is not submitted to the Lordship of Jesus, now is the time to ask His truth to transform you and set you free, to continue living a life of your calling.

Reading the Bible doesn't mean your battle is over. Just like Daniel, he prayed and continued to face opposition in his prayers. God sent the angels to fight for him. As you remain in God's word and renew your mind daily, you will be transformed. The truth shall set you free, to live a life of freedom.

APPLICATION
Think about the things that you have been battling with. Take your freedom as a daughter of the Most High God. In your quiet time ask Jesus to set you free and fill you with peace, to be ready for transformation by his truth. Ask for His power to walk in absolute freedom.

PRAYER
Dear, my precious Father, thank You for completing me with Your truth and taking everything which overwhelms me. I'm not a slave to sin, fear or addiction. Today I choose to walk in freedom and be who You called me. I'm a vessel that will transform the lives of many other women

as I continue to live in the freedom You've given me.

In Jesus name, amen.

Further scriptures
John 14:15
Psalm 119:11

Use this space to journal your thoughts

Use this space to journal your thoughts

Day 23
Learn to let go and let God in

Psalm 51
Create in me a pure heart and steadfast spirit within me.

When life brings us to a season of disappointment and challenges, it can distance our love relationship with the Father and isolate us. It's not always easy to let go of pain and hurt. As women, we carry people in our hearts. Some women get too scared to be in relationships to avoid disappointment and hurt.

Today's devotion reminds us of the heart of the Father. He wants us to let go of everything which has disappointed us and let Him in. As we learn to let God into our situation we will feel freedom and peace in our hearts that will help us to love again and be able to pursue the things God wants us to pursue with His wisdom.

I hear God say, "Let me take over your situation and everything that is heavy on you and allow me to take control."

Life has challenges and difficulties, but there is nothing difficult for God to change as we Let God in over the situation. He can change our pain into praise and our worry into worship.

APPLICATION
As you put on worship music today and allow God's peace over your situation, ask the Holy Spirit to come and fill you with peace. Allow Him into your heart again to give you peace that surpasses all understanding. As you are still, ask Jesus to restore your love for those who hurt or disappointed you. As you finish this prayer, ask Jesus to forgive you for carrying things in your heart and for grace to forgive those who have wronged you.

PRAYER

Dear, precious Father, I pray for You to come and I make room in my heart; for You to bring peace, love, patience, kindness, and all fruits of the Spirit. I invite You into my heart. I ask You to come in and take everything inside of my heart that is not of You and fill me with the things of Your kingdom to make me more like You. Teach me to love what You love and forgive those as You forgive me.

In Jesus name, amen.

Further scriptures
Isaiah 1:18-19
1Corithians 13

Use this space to journal your thoughts

Day 24
Believe in Me

1 John 5:14
And this is the confidence that we have in Him, that, if we ask anything according to His will, He hears us.

This is the confidence that we have in Him if we pray anything according to His will, He will answer us.

Jesus calls us to a place of believing, away from a place of doubting His promises. We surrender all our plans and believe in God who does the impossible, even with faith the size of a mustard seed. Today's devotion is a good reminder to look to Jesus as the one who promised all He said He would. It is the lies of the enemy, that give us the spirit of fear and doubt. Sometimes we question God and fail to believe in His promises.

I hear God saying, "Trust Me again and walk on My path. I will help you."

APPLICATION
Write down all things that God has promised in your life. As you're in a quiet time, think of a time you doubted God and felt like giving up on His promises. Ask God to restore your faith and believe Him for the promises over your life.

PRAYER
Dear, precious Father, thank You for Your promises over my life. Teach me to believe in Your promises and trust that they will come to pass. Restore my faith every time I doubt Your promises. Cause me to wait patiently and to believe that in Your time, You will fulfil all that You promised me.

In Jesus name, amen.

Further scriptures
Matthew 7:7
Hebrews 11:6

Use this space to journal your thoughts

Day 25
Do not give up

Isaiah 40:30
Those who are waiting on the Lord will renew their strength and they will fly high like an eagle.

Sometimes, we feel unworthy or unwanted and struggle with the sense of belonging. When we face rejection we might feel the only option is to give up. In today's devotional, Jesus invites you to look to Him as the author and finisher of your race. Just because it didn't work the first time, doesn't mean God will not show up again.

I hear God saying, "I know you feel tired but I'm here to give you strength to stand again and try again this time with Me."

APPLICATION
As you take a breath in, think of everything you gave up and the things you feel have been hard to trust God with. Ask Jesus to give you hope and strength to start a new beginning.

PRAYER
Dear, my precious Father, today I surrender all my plans, dreams, and all of my needs to You. Restore my hope, as I pursue the things You entrusted to me. Break every spirit of fear in me and and give me the spirit of faith to trust You again as I take steps toward a new beginning.

In Jesus name, I pray, amen.

Further scriptures
Psalm 138:7
Isaiah 40:18-19

Use this space to journal your thoughts

Day 26
I will level the mountains

Isaiah 45:2
"I will go before you and level the mountains to make the crooked places straight."

The Father's heart is to see His children live joyfully and enjoy our loving relationship with Him. His promise, as a Father, is that He will go before us and level the mountains, He will make the crooked places straight. Give it up to God, He can change our worry into worship. He changes our mountains into miracles and our battles into blessings.

I hear God saying, "For all crooked places in your life, it is a time to renounce and rebuke. Hear Me and obey, hear what I have promised." I see the picture of God's hands levelling your mountain. I see Him fixing things you have struggled to fix on your own. I see him bring peace to your heart, calling you to a place of rest.

APPLICATION
Today's devotion is a good reminder that we can give God every mountain and every battle we face. He promised to level our mountains! Write down anything you feel the enemy brings to your life or anything that feels like a mountain. As you close your eyes in quiet time ask God to give you peace that surpasses all understanding. Exchange your battles for blessings and your mountains for miracles.

PRAYER
Dear, precious Dad, thank You for the victory You gave me today. I choose to walk in authority and believe You have already won the battle for me and can level every mountain the enemy puts on my path. I am holy, victorious, and more than a conqueror.

In Jesus name, amen.

Further scriptures
Philippians 4:13
Exodus 14:14

Use this space to journal your thoughts

Day 27
Be the light

John 12:36
"While you have the light, believe in the light."

We live in a world full of darkness. Sometimes, things come in the form of light but after we open the door, the enemy pushes his darkness upon us. We can start to live a life unworthy of our calling. Today's word, reminds us we're the 'light of the world' and we need to believe in the light and live a life that reflects our calling.

I hear God say, He has set you apart from the things of this world and He wants you to live a life worthy of your calling. You can be that vessel for fruitful work. When there is light, darkness disappears. Be the 'light of the world,' so that people can see God, who works inside you!

APPLICATION
Think of something in your life that is not reflecting God's light. Ask God to give you strength to walk in the light and cast out all things of no authority over you.

PRAYER
Dear precious Father, help me to live a life that reflects Your glory so that people can see Your light shine through me in everything I do. I want to be a holy and acceptable vessel, used by you to reflect your light wherever I go.

In Jesus name, amen.

Further scriptures
Matthew 5:16
Isaiah 60:1

Use this space to journal your thoughts

Day 28
The Lord is my Rock and Fortress

Psalm 18:2
The LORD is my Rock, my Fortress and my Deliverer; my God is my Rock, in Whom I take refuge.

Today's word reminds you that you are a child of the Mighty Lord; who is your rock and fortress. He is your deliverer in times of trouble where you can take refuge. Many times life brings challenges and difficulties that make us feel alone. God's word today reminds us that even if people are not on your side, God will be on your side. You can trust Him and believe He will never leave or forsake you. He will be your Deliverer in times of trouble even when everyone walks away.

I hear God say, "I want you to fully surrender your life to Me. I will make your path straight. My hand is mighty to save you."

APPLICATION

Today's devotional is a reminder for every battle that you have been fighting alone, God wants you to shout loud with a voice of praise! "I am more than a conqueror. I am free, as greater is He that is in me, than he who is in this world!" Declare victory in every arena of your life, as you receive God's power to help you overcome all battles you have been fighting.

PRAYER

Dear, precious Daddy, thanks for being my Fortress and my Strong Tower. I can trust You in all situations I am facing. Thanks for always being on my side when people turn against me. I choose to trust You from today and give all my battles to You.

In Jesus name, amen.

Further scriptures
Psalm 62:6
2 Samuel 22:2

Use this space to journal your thoughts

Day 29
Nothing is impossible

Luke 1:37
"With God nothing is impossible."

Often, we go through difficulties in life and face challenges that make us forget the power of God in our lives. The story of Lazarus is a good reminder of this. Lazarus's sisters gave up because Jesus didn't show up when they needed Him. They thought there was nothing Jesus could do because their brother had died. Lazarus was truly dead. God knew Jesus would soon be with Mary and Martha as they wept. He also knew that Jesus would resurrect Lazarus in a mighty way. We are like Mary and Martha in that we don't always understand God's plan and perhaps forget, that He is the life-giver, the healer and the most glorious God Almighty.

Today's devotion is a good reminder for you to trust the power of God, especially in your worst situation. Even when life feels stagnant or painful, Jesus can turn it around. He will always be glorified. Nothing is impossible to Him.

I hear God saying, "Give Me all the impossible situations you struggle with. Give Me all things that look dead In your life, and trust Me to turn your situation around!"

APPLICATION
Think of the things you feel you've given up on or that seem impossible. Write them down and as you breathe in and out, I want you to declare life and freedom over your situation!

PRAYER
Dear, my precious Daddy, thank You for Your peace that surpasses all understanding. Today I declare victory, peace, and freedom over my life and believe in Your power to change, heal, and

deliver. I know that all things are possible for You and that You can turn my situation around.

In Jesus name, amen.

Further scriptures
Luke 18:27
Exodus 4:1-3

Use this space to journal your thoughts

Day 30
Learn from me

Matthew 11:29
"Take My yoke upon you, and learn of Me; for I am meek and lowly in heart: and ye shall find rest unto your souls."

Jesus told us to, 'rest in Him.' When we withdraw from Him and stop resting, we lose our peace. Jesus reminds us He wants us to learn from Him. To stay close and rest in Him, always. I sense in today's devotion, Jesus is inviting you to learn from Him. He is meek and lowly in heart and wants to transfer this to you for your soul to have a permanent rest, no matter what you face in life. The more we learn the heart of the Father, the more we will receive rest in our souls.

APPLICATION
Think of how you can learn to allow God to be in charge of your life, even when you face difficult situations. You can always choose to rest in Him and learn to depend on Him fully, allowing Him to take control of your situation. Think of the moments you allowed your heart to be troubled and didn't allow Jesus to calm your storm. Ask for forgiveness and pray for God to teach you to be more like Jesus.

PRAYER
Dear my precious Father, teach me to learn from You and walk in the way You have called me to walk. Give me a meek spirit like You, Jesus, so I can learn to rest in You, no matter what I face throughout life.

In Jesus name, amen.

Further scriptures
Romans 12:2
John 14:27

Use this space to journal your thoughts

Day 31
Rejoice in Me

Philippians 4:4
Rejoice in the Lord always: and again I say, Rejoice.

God calls us to rejoice in Him. We rejoice because the joy of the Lord is our strength. David wrote about finding rest in the Lord's salvation. Joy is found in Jesus and the eternal promises of God. Even when you go through the valley of the shadow of death, you shall not fear any evil because greater is He that is in you than he who is in this world.

I hear God say, "My joy is available for you. I am eternal and My promises are eternal. Find strength and peace in Me and you will always rejoice."

APPLICATION
Today's devotion is about choosing to rejoice in God, all the time. Play a worship song that speaks about rejoicing in God; praising Him for who He is and what He has already done in your life.

PRAYER
Dear, precious Daddy, thank You for who You are and what You have done in my life. Today, I choose to rejoice in You even though I don't understand what You are doing in my life. I choose to rejoice in You all the time.

In Jesus name, amen.

Further scriptures
Nehemiah 8:14
Psalm 23:4

Use this space to journal your thoughts

Day 32
Trust My ways not yours

Isaiah 55:8
"For My thoughts are not your thoughts, neither are your ways My ways," saith the Lord.

We often have opportunities or find ourselves in situations where we feel confused and wonder if it is God's will. If things don't go to plan, we must remember to declare that His will be done, not ours. In today's devotional, God reminds us to give all our plans to Him. His ways are not our ways but if we submit to His will, we will find peace and strength to continue. I sense God is inviting you today, to learn to submit to His will. If anything is overwhelming, submit it to God, who will help and lead you on the right path.

APPLICATION
What do you dream of and desire? Write down the things God has already accomplished in your life. As you trust God to lead you in His will, commit your dreams and plans to Him and trust Him to lead you on the right path.

PRAYER
Dear, precious Father, thanks for the plans You have for me. Today I commit all my plans to You and invite You to take control. I surrender all my plans and dreams to You and believe You will accomplish all You have promised.

In Jesus name, amen.

Further scriptures
Psalm 32:8
Jeremiah 29:11

Use this space to journal your thoughts

Day 33
Don't forget who you are

1 Peter 2:9
But ye are a chosen generation, a royal priesthood, a holy nation, a peculiar people; that ye should show forth the praises of Him who hath called you out of darkness into his marvellous light.

God calls you holy, a royal priesthood and a peculiar person. This is your identity. Don't allow the enemy to speak negative words or condemnation into your heart. When God calls us holy, He looks at us with His eyes and sees we're holy and accepted. Do not allow the enemy to condemn you or make you feel unworthy. Know who you are and who God called you to be. He crafted you; you're beautifully and wonderfully made in His image. You are holy. You are beautiful. You are chosen. You are special. That's who you are.

I hear God saying, "You are My beloved, I love you just as you are. Today I want you to know you are worthy, acceptable, holy and special. I want you to know I created you beautifully for My glory. I want to use you mightily to reflect My glory in this world."

APPLICATION
Think of the false identity the enemy uses to condemn you. I want you to write down how God sees you and declare it over your life.

PRAYER
Dear, precious Father, I know you love me more than I can imagine. I feel Your love even during my mistakes or when I do things that are not pleasing to You. Today, I want to accept my identity, live according to Your will and know who I am. I'm a holy and acceptable vessel, ready to be used for Your glory. Help me to be more like You, Jesus.

In Jesus name, amen.

Further scriptures
Psalm 139
Jeremiah 31:3

Use this space to journal your thoughts

Day 34
The best is yet to come

Proverbs 23:18
There is surely a future hope for you and your hope will not be cut off.

It's God's will for us to believe in His promises. Today, Jesus wants to open your eyes, to imagine the future that He has for you. The enemy will try to bring confusion and discourage you. When things are not going according to your plan, it does not mean God is not covering you in grace. Trust God's plan and know that He can make all things work together for His good.

I hear God saying, "Trust me, I have the best plan for you and all I promised shall come to pass.

Continue to trust in Me and wait on Me patiently. I have many blessings in store for you."

APPLICATION
Think of when the enemy has tried to steal your joy and your attention has moved away from God's promises. I want you to write down the promises God has over your life. In your quiet time, I want you to ask Jesus to restore your peace and strength, whilst waiting on His promises.

PRAYER
Thank You, Lord, for the best plans You have for me. I declare all the blessings that You promised over my life to come to pass. I rebuke every voice of the enemy which brings confusion. I receive all You have for me in faith and trust You will accomplish Your promises in my life.

In Jesus name, amen.

*Further scriptures
Matthew 21:22
2 Corinthians 5:7*

Use this space to journal your thoughts

Day 35
Seek to know Me

Matthew 6:33
"But seek ye first the kingdom of God, and His righteousness; and all these things shall be added unto you."

The Father's heart always pursues us, to bring us closer to Him in a loving relationship. As women, we have many things on our minds. Even when it's time to draw closer to God, our minds might work overtime or we try to figure things out on our own and miss the opportunity to spend time with the Father.

Just like Martha when she was busy in the kitchen trying to think of the best thing to do, she forgot

Jesus was there to spend quality time with. You might be like Martha today, but Jesus is inviting you to His feet and to get to know Him; just like Mary took her quality time spent with Jesus. The quality time you spend with Jesus changes your worry into worship.

I hear God saying to you, "Seek to know Me and I will give you the desires of your heart. Learn from Me and I will accomplish all I promised you."

APPLICATION
Think of everything you attempt to do alone and spend time at the feet of Jesus. Ask Jesus to forgive you for spending time on your own, missing the opportunity to worship Him. Play a worship song and enjoy quality time with Jesus.

PRAYER
Dear, precious Daddy, today I want to surrender my life to You and want to seek more of You, more than anything. I pray You will give me the desire to spend time with You. I believe everything shall be added to me, as I seek Your kingdom first.

In Jesus name, amen.

Further scriptures
Psalm 105:4
Hebrew 11:6

Use this space to journal your thoughts

Day 36
Give Me your burden

Psalm 55:22
Cast your burden on the Lord and he shall sustain you.

God invites us to give Him our pain, burdens, hurt, and all disappointment. He promises to sustain us in difficulties. As women, many have the wrong version of how we think God created us, to be strong and a need for us to be resilient. We believe we should carry everything in our hearts because we can do so.

Just because you are strong, does not mean you need to depend on your strength to control things.

This is why, in today's devotional, David encourages us to cast our burden on the Lord.

I hear God today, inviting you to be in a place of surrender and learning, to give Him your burden because He cares for you.

APPLICATION
Today, think of something you face in this season which is a burden. I want you to give it to Jesus. Ask Him to exchange your burden and give you the garment of praise.

PRAYER
Lord Jesus, thank you for exchanging my burden with Your garment of praise. From today, I will trust You to carry everything, that is too heavy on me. I'll learn to give to You, all my fear, my pain, my disappointment, and exchange it with Your praise.

In Jesus name, amen.

Further scriptures
Philippians 4:6-7
Isaiah 46:4

Use this space to journal your thoughts

Day 37
Draw near to Me

James 4:8
Draw near to God, and He will draw near to you. Cleanse your hands, you sinners; and purify your hearts, you double-minded.

In today's devotional, God invites us to draw near to Him. When we make mistakes, often we think God is judging us. We must run straight to Him. God's love is pure and unending. He is forgiving and merciful.

I hear God's saying to you today, "Come as you are. I loved you with everlasting love. There is nothing that separates Me from you. I invite you into My presence. Anything that troubles your heart, that makes you run from Me, I will help you overcome and transform you into who I called you to be. Holy and blameless. My special vessel that I set apart to bring My glory."

APPLICATION
Think of something that seems like an obstacle or causes you to mess up. Any addiction or sin that makes you feel unconfident to go into God's presence. He invites you to go to Him as you are and bring anything that takes away your confidence of being called His beloved. He wants to purify you and set you free.

PRAYER
Dear, precious Father. I invite You into my life today. I have been trying to draw near to You but my sins make me feel I don't deserve Your love. Today, I accept Your love and Your forgiveness. Help me to be more like You, Jesus and live a life worthy of my calling.

In Jesus name, amen.

Further scriptures
Hebrew 4:16
Hebrew 10:22

Use this space to journal your thoughts

Day 38
I love you with unending love

Jeremiah 31:3
The Lord hath appeared of old unto me, saying, "I have loved thee with an everlasting love: therefore with lovingkindness have I drawn thee."

God doesn't say, "What can you offer Me, in exchange for My love?" He is the first to love us and His love is unending. There's nothing you can do for God to love you more or love you less. His love is pure and unconditional. God loves you just as you are. Nothing you do will make Him love you more or love you less.

I hear God saying, "Come to me, I have all you need. I see the emptiness or longing for love which sometimes causes you to mess up. I can give you more than this world can offer. Receive My life and walk with it, you will be satisfied and have everlasting joy."

APPLICATION

Think of when you struggled to receive God's love because of a mistake you made. Ask God to give you pure love for Him and enable you to walk in His love always, so that you can overcome all the plans of the enemy that come to steal and destroy your relationship with Him.

PRAYER

Dear, precious Father, today I pray You will remind me of how much You love me so that I will never forget Your unconditional love for me. Help me, stand still in my faith and show my love to You, in all seasons of my life and not forget who I am; Loved and separated for You.

In Jesus name, amen.

Further scriptures
Psalm 51
Isaiah 1:8

Use this space to journal your thoughts

Day 39
Hear My voice

John 10:27
"My sheep hear My voice, and I know them, and they follow Me."

We hear many voices in this world. Some voices cause us not to hear God. Sometimes, we hear our own voices and make choices that lead to destruction. Other times, the voice of the enemy leads us into temptation and then we blame ourselves or those around us. Today, Jesus invites us to be in a loving relationship with Him, so that we can hear His voice clearly when He speaks. When we open our inner ears to hear God's voice, we see His beauty and feel the joy to follow His leads into His will.

I hear God saying, "Open your ear to hear My voice, I am gentle and humble. I will teach you how you should go, to help you live according to My will."

APPLICATION
Write down any moments you listened to your own voice or the voice of the enemy, that led you to make the wrong decision. As you're in a quiet time, ask the Holy Spirit to help you listen to His voice and obey; so that you can do what is pleasing and honourable to the Father.

PRAYER
Dear, my precious Father, today I invite you into my life to be my good shepherd and to be able to hear Your voice. I repent for every moment I listen to my voice and the voice of the enemy, that led me to make bad choices or sin against You. Holy Spirit, help me to hear Your voice clearly and follow Your lead.

In Jesus name, amen.

Further scriptures
John 10:14
Revelation 3:20

Use this space to journal your thoughts

Day 40
You are free indeed

Galatians 5:1
Stand fast therefore in the liberty wherewith Christ has made us free, and be not entangled again with the yoke of bondage.

As you finish the last day of your devotion, you should see it's God's grace that will help you to live a life worthy of your calling. He will not allow any plans of the enemy to destroy and steal the big plans He has for you. No sickness, disappointment, or temptation will separate you from the love relationship with the Father. Christ has set you free. You are free indeed.

I hear God saying, "My truth will continue to transform you, remain in Me, and know I have a good plan for you. Don't forget who you are, you are holy and acceptable. You are victorious and more than a conqueror. Christ is in you as the hope of glory. In Him, you live, breathe, and have all your needs fulfilled."

APPLICATION
Today I want you to declare victory and believe you are more than a conqueror through Christ who gives you strength. There is nothing that can stop God's plans for your life. You will continue to dwell in His presence and allow His truth to transform your daily life.

In Jesus name, amen.

Further scriptures
2 Corinthians 3:17
Psalm 118:5

Use this space to journal your thoughts

REFLECTIONS

Reflect on the 40-day journey, get to know the truth of the word that will draw you closer to the heart of the Father and walk in the freedom you learnt from this devotional book.

I trust you feel the transformation in your mind, soul, and heart after walking a 40-day journey of transformation with Jesus.

Be like Jesus, who overcame temptation during His time on the mountain, seeking the heart of the Father and changed the world after finishing His prayers.

I believe you will be transformed by the truth. Go and change the world. Be the woman God called you to be and live a victorious life daily.

Blessings,
Tabitha.

Connect with me:
tabbytommy@gmail.com

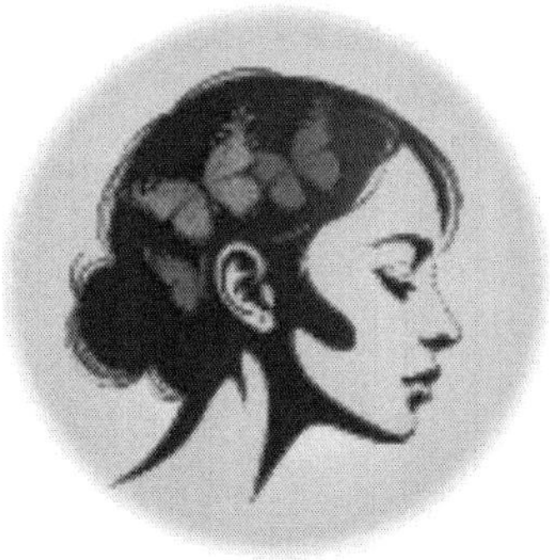

Made in the USA
Middletown, DE
05 November 2024